To Molly
(A real friend)

The Bristol
Treasure Island Trail

The Long John Silver Trust

Best Wishes

Mark x

Layout design Sally Mundy

This edition published in 2005 by
Broadcast Books
84 Whiteladies Road
Bristol
BS8 2QP

www.broadcastbooks.co.uk

This book is dedicated
to the memory of
Frank Shipsides esq. M.A.
1908 - 2005

The Pirate King
— almost —

The Treasure Island Trail

This book has been produced by *The Long John Silver Trust*,
co-founded by Mark Steeds and Gerry Brooke (Chairman)
Written and researched by Mark Steeds (Secretary/Treasurer)
Photographs from the Long John Silver Trust collection
Additional Research by Gerry Brooke and Dru Marland
Illustrations of ships by Dru Marland
Cover and Treasure Island Trail Map by Adrian Blenkiron

Pirate Lee enjoying The Great Reading Adventure

As part of the Great Reading Adventure, organised by Bristol City Council two years ago, free, abridged copies of Treasure Island were distributed to every school in the city.

An enjoyable time was had by all when Hawkesbury Primary School in South Gloucestershire kindly allowed Herbie Rawlings and Mark Steeds, from the Long John Silver Trust, to read Stevenson's exciting novel to the whole school. By re-instating dialogue left out of the abridged version, favourite characters came vividly to life. Herbie's renditions of Blind Pew, complete with sinister cockney accent, plus Ben Gunn with his high pitched "Cheese I likes ...." were the highlights.

In fact it went so well that, when the BBC recently serialised a new adaptation of Stevenson's Kidnapped, Hawkesbury School invited the duo back for another rendition.

To the Hesitating Purchaser

This booklet has been produced to help support a campaign being led by the *Long John Silver Trust* to create a **Treasure Island Trail**. The Trustees are a group of local individuals who believe passionately in the project and the benefits it could bring to both Bristol and the South West, and have worked hard to form the Trust and achieve Registered Charity status.

Our aims are to commission, erect and maintain an iconic sculpture of Long John Silver, one of Bristol's most famous fictional characters, and establish a Treasure Island Trail of sculptures along the waterfront from King Street to Prince Street Bridge (where currently there are no waterside sculptures). We want the Trail to be enjoyed by people on foot or afloat, and also to tell the story in sequence, so careful thought has been given to their positioning. To make the Trail even more educational and inclusive we would also like to commission a "Pirate Boat" that will enable parties of school children and disabled people to experience the story of *Treasure Island* in a unique way.

To do this the Trust proposes seven sculptural works of art, which will cover all the principal events and characters from the classic novel. In the meantime, the trail has been laid out in this book and we hope it will be followed and enjoyed by many. Once the Trail is complete we would also like to engage with Bristol's Performing Arts Schools to help bring the concept to life.

Apart from showing the initial thinking behind the Trail, this book explores some of the characters from Bristol's 300 year privateering past and their influence on writers such as Daniel Defoe and Robert Louis Stevenson. The Trust aim to have the Trail ready for 2008, which will be the 125th Anniversary of Treasure Island's publication, and the 300th Anniversary of Woodes Rogers' epic voyage.

`Yo Ho Ho and a Boat Load of Fun!

The Mervyn Peake Trust

When Bristol City Council launched the *Great Reading Adventure* in 2003, they produced an excellent booklet that showed the work of nearly every illustrator that ever worked on *Treasure Island*. By far the most dramatic and memorable of all these images were those done by Mervyn Peake. These provided the inspiration for the foundation of the Long John Silver Trust, so that when a Treasure Island Trail was first proposed, Mervyn Peake's illustrations immediately came to mind, paving the way for a feasible interpretation of the book in sculpture form.

When further looking into the accomplishments of Mervyn Peake it became instantly apparent that the man was a genius. Not only was he a great illustrator; he was an artist, poet and novelist, famed for his *Nonsense Poems* and other children's books, most notably *Gormenghast*.

The Trust contacted Mervyn's son, Sebastian, who shares his father's admiration for Robert Louis Stevenson and Treasure Island and is a most enthusiastic supporter of the Treasure Island Trail. Sebastian and the Mervyn Peake Trust have very generously allowed us to use some of those glorious illustrations in this book.

Sebastian told us that as a young boy in Sark, just after the war, he was used as Jim Hawkins' model, vividly recalling posing on the kitchen table in winter with just a smelly old oil stove for warmth. Another memory was his father's ability to quote verbatim any passage requested from *Treasure Island*.

The proposed 'coming to life' of Stevenson's wonderfully colourful characters in a sculpture trail for the city's harbourside has the enthusiastic backing of the Mervyn Peake family and Trust. We hope that the concept will be equally inspirational to others, and provide a lasting tribute to perhaps the best children's story ever written.

The Long John Silver Trust

Acknowledgements

Grateful thanks are due to the following for their help, support and enthusiasm:

Sebastian Peake	Redcliffe Press
Fiona Steeds	Akeman Press
Bristol Evening Post	Bristol Record Office
Wickwar Brewery	Bristol Central Library
Radio Bristol	Clifton Bookshop, Whiteladies Road
Penny Marketing	Anne and Jerry Hicks
Bristol Magazine	Hawkesbury Primary School
Jungle Talk	Hawkesbury Show
Bristol Savages	Princess of Wales, Bedminster
Bristol CAMRA	Pirate Pete
Bristol Ferry Boat Co.	Louise Roberts
Mathew Project	Herbie Rawlings

A big *Thank You* to all the Friends of the Long John Silver Trust for their valued help and loyal support.

Nicholas Pocock's *A view from Sea Banks towards St. Mary Redcliffe* pai

...cock was a Bristol sea captain and Britain's first great maritime artist.

What is a Pirate?

What do we think of when we hear the word 'pirate'? A picture-book blackguard, complete with cutlass and jolly roger? Piracy must be one of the oldest crimes, and a pirate is actually anyone who robs or plunders at sea, or sometimes from the shore. Pirates usually target other ships, but have been known to attack targets on shore.

Since at least the 19th century, pirates have been recognized as *"hosti humanis generis"* (enemies of the human race). It is not often realized that piracy is still going on in many parts of the world, and, far from going away, is actually on the increase. Unlike the old time pirates, most of today's pirates get about in nippy speedboats. They're more likely to be wearing balaclavas than bandannas, and using AK- 47 assault rifles rather than cutlasses.

Piracy upon the high seas today is a prosecutable offence under international law. Seaborne piracy against merchant vessels remains a great problem (estimated worldwide losses are eight to ten billion pounds per year), particularly in the waters between the Pacific and Indian oceans, and specifically in the straits of Malacca and Singapore, which are used by over 50,000 commercial ships a year, the Red Sea and along the East Africa coast. Ships docking at Avonmouth and Portbury today may very well have experienced piracy attacks or threats when passing through these perilous waters.

For a long time the prosecution of piracy was a tricky business, because piracy on the high seas is not within the legal jurisdiction of any state. This means that countries can technically only prosecute any pirates they catch not on behalf of themselves, but for the 'common good'. In practice however, just as in centuries before, a country will only go to the trouble of prosecuting pirates if their own ships are being threatened.

Piracy and the West Country

The West Country has had links with piracy for at least 1000 years. The first mention of acts of piracy seems to have been in 915, when a Viking raid from Brittany sailed into the Bristol Channel and ravaged Herefordshire, until they surrendered to the Saxons. Guards were set on the South coast from Cornwall to the Avon to prevent the vikings from landing, and they were forced to remain on Flatholme, many starving to death, until a favourable wind finally allowed them to escape to Ireland. A century later in 1068 another raid of Vikings came from Ireland into the mouth of the

Avon and ravaged the countryside, even rowing up to Bristol. However the Bristolians repulsed them and they sailed away again.

Pirates on Lundy

The next major spate of piracy in the South West was headed by Sir William de Marisco, who murdered a king's messenger at his manor at Portishead in 1235. He was outlawed and escaped to Lundy Island, which his family owned. Lundy was to have a regular and ever-changing pirate population: Marisco's descendents ravaged the ships of the Bristol channel for the next century, until the clan leader was finally captured by the soldiers of Henry III and dragged at the end of a horse's tail to Bristol and then on to London, where he was executed as a traitor. In the 1440s Colyn Dolphyn, a Breton pirate, used Lundy as a base until finally he ran ashore in Glamorgan and was executed by being buried up to his neck in Tresilian Sands near St Donats.

During the 16th and 17th centuries, Lundy was used as a base by Barbary Corsairs from North Africa. They were pioneered by Murat Rais, an Albanian known for his ferocity, who had been elevated to "Captain of the Seas" by the Sultan of Algiers. Murat Rais led his Corsairs out of their former stronghold in the Mediterranean up the coast of France and into the Bristol Channel, taking a heavy toll on the ships plying between Bristol, Ireland and the West Indies, and even lying in wait for merchant ships off Denny Island, off Portishead. Many English people were carried off as slaves to row their galleys home to North Africa. On the other side of the coin any captured Corsairs would be brought to Bristol and chained to the harbour wall at the Gib Tayler, a large dockside crane opposite the Ostrich pub, and left to drown as the incoming tide crept up the walls.

However the criminal activity was not all one way: The sailors of Bristol and the South West have themselves had a long history of shady dealings. To avoid the government's heavy import duties on luxury goods such as tobacco and rum, smuggling was for a long time a normal way of doing things for Bristol merchants. They would keep two sets of books; one for goods upon which duty had been paid, and one for the contraband, and a smuggler might readily cross the line from smuggling to piracy if the opportunity arose. Government officials trying to catch the smugglers red-handed in their activities on the lonely coasts of Somerset and North Devon were extremely unpopular with the locals, as whole communities benefited from the trade in contraband.

Contemporary shipping from the Golden Age

Spanish Galleon: 500 tons, 18 gu
strong, fast and manoeuverable. T
Manila galleons, as classed by Rog
could be up to 2000 tons.

The Prey: a *Merchantman*, 280 tons,
20 crew, 4 guns.

Brigantine: 150 ton, 100 crew, 10 cannon. Popular with pirates; the Navy used them too. They could also be rowed with sweeps (oars) through the gunports if becalmed.

Schooner: 100 ton, narrow hull, shallow draft, 8 cannon, 75 crew, 4 swivel guns, 11 kts. Popular with pirates in the caribbean and N America.

Sloop: 100 tons, 8ft draft, 11 kts, 14 cannon, 75 crew, fast and shallow - drafted, an ideal pirate vessel.

A Pirate's Vocabulary.

Buccaneer This comes from "boucan", a wooden frame which was used for cooking meat by hunters in the Caribbean. They became known as as boucaniers and when they took to piracy, took the name with them.

Corsair This name derives from the Latin word "Cursa" means a raid, or expedition. These pirates, operating mostly in the Mediterranean, included the Moslem Barbary corsairs from the North African coast, with their strongholds in Tunis, Tripoli and Algiers. They operated from the times of the Crusades until 1816, when the bombardment of Algiers saw the last of them. The most famous Barbary Corsair was Barbarossa.

There were also Christian corsairs who operated out from Malta from the times of the Crusades onwards, 'legitimised' by "letters of marque" issued by the Knights of St John. Any Muslim Turks captured by the Christian Corsairs were forced into the hellish life of rowing the galleys of the Knights of St. John as slaves. It required 1000 slaves to man all the galleys of the Order, making Malta a veritable slave market until well into the eighteenth century.

Freebooter This was another word for pirate, and derives from the Dutch word "vrijbuiter" - *vrij* meaning free and *buit* meaning booty.

Pirate This comes from the Latin "pirata", which means to attack, or assault.

Privateer These men would carry a "letter of marque" from their governments, giving them permission to attack vessels belonging to the nation named in the letter, and, importantly, granting them immunity from punishment. The immunity conferred by such a letter, should the privateer be captured was, of course, questionable. Granting of "letters of marque" enabled a country to wage covert warfare. Sir Francis Drake, a famous privateer, was considered by the Spanish to be nothing but a pirate.

Instructions for privateers were issued by the Government and affected all such matters as manning and equipment, wearing of colours, conduct towards neutrals, procedure as to prize, ransom, disposal of prisoners, etc. Every commander had a copy of these instructions, and he was bound by them to render a copy of his journal to the Secretary of the Admiralty. Because the sailor crew were entitled to a share of the prize money - far more than a sailor could expect in wages from the navy - they did not need to be 'press-ganged', in fact a privateer could usually have his pick of sailors. Discipline was also less severe than in the navy, and often very slack indeed. As we will see from the adventures of Dampier, many a crew of privateers deserted their ships after losing patience at the non-appearance of a treasure ship whose booty they had been promised.

The Royal Navy of the early and mid18th century suffered low morale and poor leadership. An officer would be advanced by family influence, irrespective of any possible ability. A situation could and often did arise where a British merchantman (a private merchant's ship) might be taken by a French or American privateer, practically under the guns of the Royal Navy; while the more intrepid British privateers were taking the fight to the enemy in the anticipation of prizes.

Later in the century, there was a movement towards more able and humane leadership, exemplified by Admiral John Jervis, Lord St Vincent, who in turn encouraged famous admirals such as Nelson and Collingwood. By 1830, proper schemes for training the Royal Navy sailors were implemented, along with schemes for career advancement; and discipline became less brutal and arbitrary. This caused the use of the press gang to fall into disuse, though it was still legally sanctioned. With a more able and efficient Navy, the role of the privateers also became redundant.

Viking This derives from the Old Norse "vik", meaning a creek or inlet, so a Viking was someone who haunted such places

A Boucan, from which the buccaneers derived their name.

15

The most famous pirate ever came from Redcliffe, Bristol. He was Edward
Teach, alias Blackbeard. He terrorised the Caribbean and the Eastern seaboard
of the Americas from 1700 - 1718. Blackbeard came to a suitably brutal end
when he was decapitated by Lieut. Maynard, who had been sent to hunt him
down. His head swung proudly from the bowspit of Maynard's naval cutter for
the whole journey home.

Captain Woodes Rogers and the Bristol Privateers

Bristol was a prominent port for privateering and many local people became wealthy through it. Privateers were supposed to have a licence (a letter of marque) that would allow them to attack ships and commerce belonging to a hostile nation. There is a fine line between being a pirate and a privateer and Captain Kidd, who lost his political masters in England and America who had originally sanctioned his Letter of Marque, was court martialled for piracy and then horribly put to death.

In the early 17th century Bristol privateers were involved in the early colonisation of America and voyages of discovery, including some ill-fated searches for the North West Passage. Later privateers were extremely useful to the English government in actions against the French and Spanish, especially in the Caribbean.

One of the most successful privateers of all time was Captain Woodes Rogers. He was born in Bristol in 1679, the son of a successful sea captain. In 1708 he was made Commander of a sailing venture backed by the Bristol Corporation. Armed with a letter of marque which enabled him to legitimately attack Spanish and French ships, he sailed off down the coast of South America with fellow West Countryman Dampier as his pilot (navigator). They explored the Falkland Islands, rounded the Horn and nearly froze to death, then rescued the castaway Alexander Selkirk. After many successful raids on Spanish colonies where the ladies were liberated of their gold jewellery "in a most genteel manner", his little fleet of three ships returned home intact, with Woodes Rogers slightly less so: he had suffered a bullet in the mouth and a huge wooden splinter in his heel. Woodes Rodgers had became one of only three Englishmen to ever capture a Spanish treasure ship - an almost un-heard of feat - the others being Thomas Cavendish and Lord Anson a century earlier. Anson had a fleet of six naval ships and could only bring one home, making Woodes Rogers' achievement all the more remarkable.

The welcome home disintegrated into lawsuits, with many of his crew press-ganged onto other ships. Rogers even lost his home in Queen's Square for a while. It was to try and raise money that Rogers published a book based around his thrilling captain's log, *A Cruising Voyage around the World*. It became a bestseller, and inspired a host of similar adventure narratives. Woodes Rogers ended his eventful life as Governor of the Bahamas, which had become a virtual pirates' republic. He not only got the pirates pardoned by the Crown but persuaded them to fight off the Spanish, to make the colony succeed. He made many enemies and died mysteriously in 1732, possibly by poisoning. However, a grateful colony erected a statue to their governor, which stands in Nassau to this day.

Dampier, who had been Woodes Rogers' pilot, also published an account of his bucanneering exploits. They were avidly read by the public, including both Daniel Defoe and Jonathon Swift. In fact Swift actually had Gulliver refer to Dampier as his cousin in his immortal classic, *Gulliver's Travels*.

It is widely known that Alexander Selkirk was rescued by Woodes Rogers and that his story was to be embellished into what could be called the first ever English novel, *Robinson Crusoe* by Daniel Defoe. What is not so well known is that Selkirk was also the inspiration for Robert Louis Stevenson's cheese-loving character, Ben Gunn.

Bristol privateers continued to find fame and fortune on the high seas: one successful voyage in 1744 yielded so many prizes it needed 45 wagons loaded with treasure to transport it from Old Market Street to London. At its peak in the mid 1750s Bristol's privateers boasted around 40 ships, 7500 adventurers and between 1200 and 1400 guns.

Understandably, records on pirates and piracy are a little more obscure than those of their privateering cousins. Information usually came either from their victims or the pirates' pursuers. Captain Johnson (believed to be a pseudonym of Daniel Defoe) in his *General History of Ye Pyrates* gave graphic accounts and accurate statistics from both sources. For example, when talking about "Black Bart" Roberts - the famous Welsh pirate captain - he tells of the terrible fate that befell the African slaves that he had captured and the composition of his crew that ended up in Execution Dock.

Interestingly, of the 53 men that were hanged on that occasion, 26 of them were from the West Country, including 6 from Somerset (two of whom were from Minehead) and 4 from Bristol. One of the most fascinating chapters in Johnson's book is his account of Blackbeard and his fiendish exploits, and it is no surprise to learn that Robert Louis Stevenson had a copy in his collection and equally that he chose to set *Treasure Island* in Bristol.

The following vignettes illustrate fully the rich and varied role Bristol played both in the factual and fictional story of pirates.

A CRUISING

VOYAGE

ROUND THE

WORLD:

First to the SOUTH-SEAS, thence to the EAST-INDIES, and homewards by the Cape of GOOD HOPE.

Begun in 1708, and finish'd in 1711.

CONTAINING

A JOURNAL of all the Remarkable Transactions; particularly, Of the Taking of *Puna* and *Guiaquil*, of the *Acapulco* Ship, and other Prizes; An Account of *Alexander Selkirk*'s living alone four Years and four Months in an Island; and A brief Description of several Countries in our Course noted for Trade, especially in the *South-Sea.*

With Maps of all the Coast, from the best *Spanish* Manuscript Draughts.

And an INTRODUCTION relating to the *SOUTH-SEA* Trade.

By Captain *WOODES ROGERS,*
Commander in Chief on this Expedition, with the Ships *Duke* and *Dutchess* of *Bristol.*

LONDON, Printed for *A. Bell* at the Cross-Keys and Bible in *Cornhil,* and *B. Lintot* at the Cross-Keys between the two Temple-Gates, *Fleetstreet.* M DCC. XII.

Edwin Russell's sculpture of Woodes Rogers stands on the site of Fort Nassau in the Bahamas, where Woodes Rogers had his headquarters when he was Governor. The sculpture was commissioned by Sir Henry Oakes for the British Colonial Hilton in the 1930s.

William Dampier - buccaneer
An engraving of the original oil painting by Thomas Murray, 1697/8

West Country Pirates and Buccaneers
William Dampier (1651 - 1715)

The extraordinary life of one of the West Country's most famous buccaneers, William Dampier, echoes both the personal and national greed which seems to have been prevalent throughout the late sixteenth century.

It was a time of a kind of high seas free-for-all - with the English navy hardly more governed by laws, or restraint, than the multitude of marauding pirates, buccaneers and privateers who sailed off in search of Spanish treasure ships.

Europe's main sea-faring nations - chiefly Holland, France, Spain and England - were bidding to acquire as many colonies as they could. These newly-acquired lands and ports, such as existed on the Caribbean islands and South American coast, were a tremendous temptation for every sort of adventurer and rogue and very vulnerable to pirate raids.

Dampier, born into a well off farming family in 1651 at East Coker, near Yeovil, was the second of six children. When he was eighteen he was apprenticed to a seaman at Weymouth. Because of his rural upbringing he was always interested in natural history and, during his first long voyage, made an early study of prevailing winds.

Although reputedly rather cowardly by nature, he saw action at sea in the Third Anglo-Dutch war in 1673, and afterwards worked on a Jamaican sugar plantation. But, after falling out with the plantation manager, he went back to sea and later to the Bay of Campeche, in the Caribbean swamps, to work as a logswood man, the trees being sent back to Europe as a valuable source of purple dye.

Dampier, now in his early twenties, was a faithful keeper of a journal of observations. He wrote a riveting account of the region's wildlife as well as about the wild behaviour of the "Baymen" - privateers no longer employed by the British government after a peace treaty with Spain.

These "Baymen" offered him a tempting lifestyle and, realising he could earn more from pillage than from log cutting, he joined a group who planned to raid the Mexican coastal towns. He returned to England in 1678, rich enough to wed - above his station it must be added - to Judith, a duchess's maid.

Dampier was too restless, however, to settle down to domestic life and he was soon back in pirate infested Jamaica where, after buying a small Dorset estate from a trader, he joined a newly formed buccaneer fleet. With the help of Mosquito Coast indians, this ruthless gang captured the port of Portobello and then, encouraged by the success of pirate Henry Morgan several years earlier, went on to attempt a raid on silver rich Panama city. This venture ended in failure, however; the fleet broke up and there was a mass defection of crew members.

But Dampier, remaining on board ship, went on to join up with more French and English pirates. This bloodthirsty gang raided all along the Caribbean coast as well as Costa Rica, retreating periodically to the notorious buccaneer port of Tortuga.

After a quiet few months in Virginia the adventurer set off again, in 1683, on another raiding expedition. This time it was to be in the Pacific, and here he took careful naturalist notes of the islands of Juan Fernandez and the Galapagos. Hundreds of French and English freebooters joined the fleet and, rounding the Horn, they had yet another attempt at sacking Panama City, but were again repulsed, this time by Spanish warships.

Shortly afterwards Dampier joined the vessel *Cygnet* because, as his journal states, its captain, Edward Davis, would allow him to explore the Pacific. Davis had replaced Captain Swan, the original captain of the *Cygnet*. (Swan had been abandoned on a Phillipine island with part of his crew after a mutiny). The plan was for Davis and Dampier to try and intercept one of the famed Spanish treasure galleons which sailed annually from Manila to Acapulco in Mexico. But they changed tack and, in 1686, decided to sail the 6000 miles from Mexico to Guam with a crew desperately short of rations.

This hunger must have made Dampier's descriptions of the exotic foods they found in Guam and the Philippines even more mouth watering. He was the first Englishman to give descriptions of breadfruit, bananas, and plantain.

For another year, the *Cygnet* sailed the South China seas and even landed briefly, in 1688, on the shores of Australia, then called New Holland - the first English ship to do so. Dampier was bitterly disappointed by the desert wastelands he found there - at great variance with the myth that had spurred him on - that of the wonderful new undiscovered continent, Terra Australis Incognita.

Leaving the *Cygnet* anchored at Great Nicobar Island, off the Indian coast, the adventurer then set off on a terrible 130 mile journey in an outrigger

Captain Kidd was a privateer armed with a letter of Marque entitling him to attack Spanish galleons. However he turned pirate when he went after an East Indiaman (a merchant ship). His political masters in England and America lost power and he was abandoned to the Execution Dock on charges of piracy. When Dampier was court-martialled he had to pass the swinging tarred corpse of Kidd each day: a fate that could so easily have befallen him as well.

northern shores before setting sail for New Guinea, hoping to round the continent that way. Dampier found a beautiful set of green islands - which he named New Britain - before being forced by the condition of his rotting ship to set sail for home.

But the *Roebuck* only made it as far as Ascension Island where, in 1701, the vessel sank. Dampier had to hitch a ride back to England aboard an East Indiaman (a fast sailing merchant ship), along with a cargo of forty Australian plants. They were taken to Oxford where they eventually formed the core of the Sheradian herbarium.

As a result of these voyages the adventurer is commemorated today in several Australasian place names: Dampier Strait, Roebuck Bay and Dampier Land in north West Australia, and the Dampier archipelago off the western coast.

When Dampier returned, in the summer of 1702, he had to face the disgrace of a court martial instigated by the officer he had mistreated. He was found unfit for naval command, but as he'd had enough of the slender pickings of a respectable life at sea, he didn't regard this as too much of a setback.

In September 1703 he sailed off on another prospective ambushing expedition to the Pacific with his sights again on the Spanish treasure galleon sailing out of Manila. He was, this time, commodore of a ship called the *St. George*, accompanied by another, the *Cinque-Ports*. There is, unfortunately, no memoir of their unsuccessful, and shameful, attempt to ambush that elusive Spanish vessel. The disappointed sailors, who would have been given shares of the booty, all mutinied and deserted, with one departing crewman jeering "Poor Dampier, thy Case is like King James, every Body has left thee!" One of the unluckier mutineers was Scotsman Alexander Selkirk, cast off the Cinque Ports and marooned on Juan Fernandez island in November 1704. It would be many lonely years before he would be rescued by a later expedition led by Bristol seaman Woodes Rodgers and, ironically, Dampier himself.

Returning home in 1707 - after a brief stint in a Batavian prison on suspicion of piracy - Dampier had to face more allegations of ill temper, abuse of his officers, drunkenness, bribe taking and even cowardice (for refusing to board the Manila galleon) brought by his former crewmen, but astonishingly he was vindicated.

But, whatever his other failings, such was his reputation as a navigator that Dampier was recruited by Bristolian Captain Woodes Rogers for yet another

The artist Frank Shipsides' impression of the *Duke* and *Duchess* being fitted out at Redcliffe Wharf, Bristol, for Captain Woodes Rogers' expedition around the world, which was piloted by Dampier.

canoe, surviving dysentry and many other hazards, to finally arrive in Sumatra. For the next year and a half he explored Tonquin (it's now Vietnam), Malacca (now Melaka) on the Malay peninsula, and even India.

By the time that he eventually arrived home, in 1691, he had become first Englishman to have circumnavigated the globe since Thomas Cavendish, a century earlier.

Despite his adventures Dampier had not made his fortune; in fact his only possessions seem to have been his journal and a tattooed Philippino slave, 'Prince Giolo' - who died soon after going on show in London and Oxford. So, two year later Dampier was off once again, this time on a more lucrative quest. He was navigating *The Dove*, one of four ships looking for "trade" in the Caribbean.

A mutiny, however, soon turned the little fleet into a pirate one captained by Henry Avery. For once Dampier seemed to have been out of the action and he remained with *The Dove* at port in Spain, and even sued for back wages. However the High Court of Admiralty dismissed his claim and upheld the charge, that Dampier had abetted the mutiny, made by the fleet's owner. Realising that there was little loot coming his way, Dampier testified against six of his former shipmates when they were tried for piracy.

In 1697 the adventurer published *A New Voyage Round the World*, and later, by popular demand, a supplement to it. Full of blood-curdling accounts of piracy but noted more for its descriptions of the flora and fauna of the New World, as well as of its trade winds, storms and currents, the book was a great success, and Dampier found himself a popular hero, admired by merchants, statesmen, and scientists. He began to move in elevated circles and was even appointed to the well-salaried post of land-carriage man at the London Customs House. As an acknowledged expert he was called on to testify to the Board of Trade on piracy matters.

His reputation on a high, Dampier was, in 1699, given the command of *HMS Roebuck*. This was to be a scientific exploration of the Pacific plus a circumnavigation of terra Australis but the navigator had to contend with a ship that was in a terrible condition, as well as having an inexperienced and unhappy crew.

One officer had so little respect for Dampier that he insulted him on several occasions - causing the short-fused captain to cane and then imprison him. The ship finally reached Australia but, as before, only touched it's barren privateering expedition. The plan was to take two ships, *The Duke* and the *Duchess*, and try and capture (yet again) the Manila galleon. But this time they were successful and Rogers returned to England in 1711 with a shipful of Spanish loot as well as the rescued castaway, Alexander Selkirk.

Dampier retired, initially a rich man, to London, but he was sued by the owners of the ships from his previous expeditions and died in November 1714, leaving debts of £677 17s. 1d. As his will made no provision for a wife, it's possible that she had pre-deceased him.

Contemporary, and later judgements on his turbulent, but interesting life, were quite kind. In Gulliver's Travels- inspired by Dampier's accounts of strange lands - the author Jonathan Swift wrote that he was an " honest man, and a good sailor, but a little too positive in his own opinions". The poet Coleridge praised his "exquisite mind' and much later another poet, John Masefield, delighted in his descriptions of natural history as the product of a "calm, equable, untroubled and delighted vision".

Dampier's writings certainly inspired a new genre of travel writing, taken up by by Daniel Defoe and later by Robert Louis Stevenson, and his acute observations of maritime climate, tides and compass variations proved invaluable to future generations of sailors and scientists. He has been credited with being the most important explorer - before Captain Cook - to inspire interest in the South Pacific.

Contemporary illustration of a ship's worm of the sort that ate Dampier's ships. The only defence against these creatures was copper sheathing of the hull, hence "a copper-bottomed guarantee". However this often proved too expensive an investment for ships' owners.

"Admiral" Sir Henry Morgan
Buccaneer and Governor of Jamaica

Born in 1635 into a military family in Abergavenny, Wales, Morgan left school early and was shipped from Bristol to Barbados to become apprenticed as a cutler. Life as an indentured servant on the plantations did not agree with him and he escaped to serve as a subaltern on Cromwell's ship, the Western Design, which was part of Bristol Admiral William Penn's expedition that eventually conquered Jamaica in 1655.

Morgan turned buccaneer and the highlight of his career followed soon after, when he led a band of 2,000 English and French pirates in a raid on the rich Spanish-owned port of Panama. After sacking the city, Morgan returned to the Caribbean with a great treasure. He held a meeting of his fellow pirate kings on his flagship, *HMS Oxford*, but disaster struck when the vessel blew up, though sparing Morgan. The grateful Spanish attributed the event to the work of the statue of the Virgin Mary in Cartagena. Morgan was knighted by Charles II and appointed Lieutenant Governor of Jamaica. Under King's Orders, he turned on his former henchmen and associates in crime and hanged every pirate he could find.

Although he had a terrible reputation, Morgan became a respectable governor and died wealthy but childless in 1688. He had been a good administrator and founded the Jamaican town of Port Royal, which was destroyed in an earthquake a few years later.

Alexander Selkirk

Marooned sailor Alexander Selkirk, who died in 1721, is thought by many to be the inspiration behind Daniel Defoe's classic novel *Robinson Crusoe*. Born and brought up in Largo, Fife, when he was seventeen Selkirk escaped the punishments of the Scottish kirk authorities for so called "indecent" behaviour in church by running away to sea. Returning six years later, however, he soon quarrelled with his family and, in 1703, left home, but not Largo, for good.

A capable sailor and navigator he was appointed master of the privateer *Cinque Ports* under Captain Charles Pickering. Together with another vessel, *The George*, commanded by West Countryman William Dampier, the two ships left for the South Seas.

Captain Pickering, unfortunately, died en-route and was succeeded by Captain Thomas Stradling. Although Selkirk proved himself a steady and reliable seaman, especially around Cape Horn, it is probable that he formed part of a subsequent mutiny when the men got to Juan Fernandez island, off the Chilean coast. The crews had been promised rich pickings from the heavily laden Spanish galleons plying that coast. But they continued to have little success and the two commanders quarrelled to such an extent that they eventually parted company.

Selkirk and Stradling, on the *Cinque Ports*, continued sailing on around the South American coast. Eventually Selkirk decided that the ship, and its commander, were completely unfit for the voyage and declared he would rather disembark at Juan Fernandez island, where they were berthed for a refit and to take on water, than sail on any further.

He was taken at his word and left the ship, according to Woodes' Rodgers account, with "*his Clothes and Bedding, with a Firelock, some Powder, Bullets, and Tobacco, a Hatchet, a Knife, a Kettle, a Bible, some practical Pieces, and his Mathematical Instruments and Books*". The moment the vessel pulled away, however, he had a sudden change of heart and pleaded to be taken back on board. Stradling, fearing that he would lose this opportunity to get rid of the troublesome sailor, closed his ears and the *Cinque Ports* sailed off.

In his first few months on the island Selkirk went about distracted "*and had much ado to bear up against melancholy, and the Terror of being left alone in such a desolate place"*. However, the onset of winter forced him to build two huts, and faced with the challenge of survival until picked up by a passing vessel he gradually became reconciled to his fate.

He studied his Bible and began a routine of daily exercises which included singing psalms and reading the scriptures aloud. It kept up his spirits and also helped him retain the use of his speech. And so he would know which day was the Sabbath (Sunday) he also kept a calendar. He bred cats, which as well as giving him some kind of company, preserved him from the rats which gnawed constantly at his feet and clothes as he slept.

His chief amusement was to hunt goats, but after exhausting all of his powder and shot he relied on fleetness of foot to capture them. He tamed the kids to ensure a continual source of food - after all, he thought, one day he might not be able to run after them.

In his account of the four years that he spent alone on the island, Selkirk stressed the importance of two incidents. The first occurred whilst he was out hunting. Having stalked a goat to an unfamiliar part of the island, he lunged to catch the animal and the momentum carried him over the edge of an unseen precipice. The fall knocked him unconscious for at least a day and when he recovered his senses he discovered the goat dead beneath him.

Second, he was very nearly captured by Spaniards who arrived at the island in two vessels. Anxious to find out the their nationality, Selkirk was inadvertently spotted from the ships. A landing party was dispatched, and several shots fired in his direction, but Selkirk's agility allowed him to hide in the branches of a tree as his pursuers searched for him beneath.

Then, in February 1709, two Bristol privateers, the *Duke* and *Duchess*, anchored at the island for water. The *Duke* was commanded by Captain Woodes Rogers with Dampier on board as pilot.

After dark Rogers spotted a light on the island and so, the next day, sent two boats to investigate. Towards evening one returned, together with *"a Man cloth'd in Goat-Skins, who look'd wilder than the first Owners of them [who] had so much forgot his Language for want of Use, that we could scarce understand him, for he seem'd to speak his words by halves"*. The rescued man had been alone on the island for four years and four months.

Although no love was lost between them Dampier recommended Selkirk as the best man on the old *Cinque Ports* and Rogers appointed him as mate on the *Duke*. Both ships then sailed off to scour the coast of Chile. Within a

The Cock and Bottle Public-House, with Part of Messrs.
Ames and Gadd's Warehouses, Castle-Green, Bristol.

-"Nor leaves his Bottle till the Cock doth crow"

**One of Selkirk's haunts in Bristol were the inns of Cock and Bottle Lane ,
where he reputedly met Defoe.**

month a prize ship was taken, and, renamed the *Increase*, Selkirk was appointed master.

Hoping to intercept vessels sailing between Panama and Lima, Rogers led them to the Galápagos Islands for refitting before taking up positions off Cape St Lucas to await the arrival of the Spanish galleon bound for Acapulco. Low on bread, and with worms penetrating deep into their vessels' sheathing, they were about to weigh anchor when at last, a Spanish sail was sighted. The Englishmen were in luck - they were able to seize the richly laden *Nuestra Señora de la Encarnación*.

When, early in 1710, Rogers set out to cross the Pacific, a voyage of over 6000 miles, his original ships were augmented by two others. The *Nuestra Señora*, renamed the *Bachelor*, had Selkirk appointed master under Captain Thomas Dover.

The little flotilla reached Guam in March and then left for Batavia - which they sailed into in late June. Here they shared out a quantity of the booty, Selkirk acting as a commissioner. His own share was eighty pieces of eight.

Then, after refitting at Horn Island, they sailed for the Cape of Good Hope where they stayed for over three months.

In April they sailed north in a convoy of twenty-five Dutch and English ships, arriving off the Shetlands in mid July. Selkirk arrived back in London in October 1711. His extraordinary circumnavigation had taken over eight years, more than half of which had been spent alone on his island.

Selkirk was feted, wined and dined after an account of his adventures

A contemporary illustration of Defoe's *Robinson Crusoe*, which was inspired by the published castaway adventures of Alexander Selkirk.

was published by Rogers in "*A Cruising Voyage Round the World*" (1712). His rehabilitation, however, proved less successful. Coming to live in Bristol, possible with Woodes Rogers in Queen Square, we learn that an "Alexander Selkirke" of the parish of St Stephen, was wanted for an assault on Richard Nettle, shipwright, on 23 September 1713.

Some time later Selkirk returned to Largo as a recluse, constructing a cave in his father's garden. He became infatuated with a girl named Sophia Bruce, with whom, it appears, he eloped to London. It's even possible they married. In a will of January 1718, as he was about to leave, once more, for sea, Selkirk referred to Sophia as "his loveing and well beloved friend Sophia Bruce of Pellmell London, Spinster" and appointed her his executor and heir.

In October 1720 the sailor embarked on *HMS Weymouth* as master's mate and in December married a Plymouth widow called Frances Candis. He then made new will leaving everything to her. By March the following year the mariner was involved in operations against pirates on the Guinea coast and it was here, as other crew members fell sick, that he probably contracted the disease that was to kill him.

The *Weymouth's* log records Selkirk's death in December 1721. Then followed a legal battle over his estate between Frances Candis and her new husband and his first wife Sophia. The latter's bid proved unsuccessful and her fortunes eventually sank so low that she was forced to beg for parish relief.

In 1866 a tablet in honour of Selkirk was placed near his lookout on Juan Fernandez island and a bronze statue, erected some twenty years later, stands on the site of his former home in Largo. His sea chest, and a coconut shell cup, which he may have used on the island, are preserved in the national museums of Scotland.

But Selkirk's best memorial must surely be Daniel Defoe's portrait of the castaway, Robinson Crusoe, based on his life, which was published in 1719. There is some slight evidence that Defoe and Selkirk actually met, but stories that Defoe callously plundered Selkirk's journal for material, while telling its author it would never sell, are unlikely.

Daniel Defoe

Two famous writers inspired by pirate tales

Daniel Defoe and the writing of Robinson Crusoe

Built over the old dungeons of Bristol's ruinous Norman castle, in long demolished Cock and Bottle lane, there once stood a famous old pub, the Star Inn, the haunt of many of the city's characters and "convivial wits". Could it be that, drinking and smoking amongst them, if only for a short while, was that famous writer, Daniel Defoe, pricking up his ears for likely material for a planned adventure yarn? It's very possible.

Defoe had been born in London in 1660, the son of a wealthy tallow merchant. Initially intended for the life of a non-conformist minister, rarely was there such a mismatch of occupation and character. Declaring that "the pulpit is none of my office" he followed his father into commerce, but a series of highly speculative ventures ended in financial disaster with Defoe owing his creditors thousands of pounds. He was never to be out of debt for the rest of his life and wrote really to try and earn a crust.

As well as being a struggling entrepreneur, Defoe was also pamphleteer - he hated religious intolerance - a journalist, poet, spy and double agent, and a revolutionary dreamer. During his life he published well over 300 works.

For much of his remarkable life he was haunted by his creditors and by the mobs who, incensed by the content of his political pamphlets, wanted to lynch him. He was imprisoned four times. On the other hand there were periods of high favour when King William I and his court treated him like a celebrity.

While writing an account of his journeyings through southern England, Defoe ended up in hiding in Bristol, on the run once more from his London creditors. He became known as the "Sunday Gentleman" - due to his habit of only daring to show himself in public on Sundays - when no lawyer or creditor could serve legal papers on him. He struck a dashing figure, "accoutred in the fashion of the times, with a fine flowing wig, lace ruffles and a sword by his side".

Contemporary reports also mention that a drinking companion of his at the time was Alexander Selkirk (aka Robinson Crusoe), the Scottish castaway who had achieved a measure of fame some years before through the best-selling narrative of the Bristol privateer, Captain Woodes Rogers. Selkirk lived up to his fame by his habit of walking the streets clothed in his goat skins. Sworn affidavits of the period insist that "Selkirk placed his papers in Defoe's hands and that from them he wrote Robinson Crusoe". Defoe, however, denied ever meeting either Selkirk, Woodes Rodgers or that other famous West Country sea dog and travel writer, William Dampier, dismissing them all as "illiterate sailors." Nevertheless, it seems beyond doubt that his story of castaway Robinson Crusoe is based on the life of Selkirk.

Robinson Crusoe was published in April 1719 when he was about fifty-nine. Although read nowadays as an extraordinary, but straightforward, account of a castaway's amazing survival on a remote desert island, in its time the book was intended as a kind of lecture on Defoe's theories of government and religion. It was a plea for Britain's settlement and domination of new lands to be by trade rather than by military might.

Defoe was saying that English settlers could grow their coffee, spices and other crops just as effectively in Africa, only two weeks away by sail, rather than the Caribbean, a perilous ten weeks' sail away through pirate infested waters. He complained that the natural riches of soil and climate were going to waste. Even the lazy Portuguese, Defoe reminded his readers, had got around to growing coffee in Brazil.

The two best-selling publications in those days were sermons and travel books, so Defoe had not misjudged his audience. The book sold out and was then reprinted twice within two months. Defoe published a sequel and by the end of the year the two parts were published together, along with a map and six illustrations.

A year later and the story had been translated into French, Dutch and German. Although the author died of a stroke in 1731, penniless and "sinking under the Weight" of "Insupportable Sorrows", *Robinson Crusoe* has earned him the title of "The father of the English Novel."

The book, never out of print since its publication, has inspired a host of imitations. It was, without doubt, one of the inspirations for Robert Louis Stevenson's classic adventure yarn, *Treasure Island*.

A 'wanted' poster for Daniel Defoe of 1704.

"That fools look out, and knaves look on."

St. James', January 10th, 1704.

Whereas Daniel Defoe, *alias* Daniel De Fooe, is charged with writing a scandalous and seditious pamphlet, entitled *The Shortest Way with Dissenters.* He is a middle-sized, spare man, about 46 years old, of a brown complexion, but wears a wig; a hooked nose, a straight chin, gray eyes, and a mole near his mouth. A reward of £50 is offered for his apprehension.

**Robert Louis Stevenson in Davos, Switzerland,
at the time of writing *Treasure Island* in 1881.**

Robert Louis Stevenson and the writing of Treasure Island

The stirring pirate tale, *Treasure Island* by Robert Louis Stevenson, must surely rate as one of the greatest adventure stories ever written. " If this don't fetch the kids" he was to write, "Why, they have gone rotten since my day!"

As far as the author was concerned these terrifying tales of lawless pirates and buccaneers had only come to an end a century or so previously. Although Stevenson originally intended the book for a young audience, and even dedicated it to his young step-son, the book was an immediate success with readers of all ages.

Stevenson's had been a lonely and sickly childhood. The son of a Scottish lighthouse engineer and his wife, who was a rigid Calvinist, he was born in Edinburgh in 1850. His mother read him Shakespeare and the Bible and his devoted nurse fired his imagination with lurid anti-Papist tales. It was these influences that turned Stevenson into a passionate advocate of religious and cultural freedom, and his subsequent adventures as a young man certainly tested the moral tolerance of his parents. A family saga that also influenced him greatly was the fate of his two uncles - they had died trying to reclaim money and property out of which they had been swindled on the Caribbean island of St. Kitts.

The young Stevenson had a lot of time to read, and it was the popular travel narratives of the day that were to prove a direct inspiration for *Treasure Island* and it's vivid descriptions of the seafaring life. Often written by retired sea-farers, these were personal accounts of exploration in distant exotic lands coupled with blood-curdling escapades. They proved extremely popular and excited the public's curiosity about the barely explored new lands of the Americas and East Indies.

The most well-known of these accounts were written by the Somerset-born privateer, navigator and naturalist, William Dampier, and by Captain Woodes Rodgers, who lived in Bristol's Queen's Square in the early eighteenth century, and who set sail from Bristol's docks to engage in privateering (which was, in effect, government-sanctioned raids on Spanish treasure ships). These men, sometimes employed by the government, more often than not sought personal wealth through this type of licenced piracy. They survived the extreme dangers of sea battles and raids, as well as the many perils of disease and starvation that went with their life styles.

As explorers they made meticulous observations on the climates, currents, winds and tides of those new regions whose wealth they, or others, hoped to exploit. Their accounts, without doubt, provided Daniel Defoe with the inspiration to write **Robinson Crusoe**, published in 1719, a book certainly read by the young Stevenson.

Stevenson, having survived his own childhood perils, grew into a flamboyant and non-conformist young man, reluctantly studying, at his father's insistence, the law. He was quite tall but very thin, suffering intermittently from a tuberculosis-like illness which was often to threaten his life. His many friends loved him for his vitality, charm and brilliant conversation as he paced ceaselessly to and fro, constantly smoking cigarettes.

He sometimes wore a dark blue pirate cloak fastened with a snake buckle, and spent the little allowance his parents gave him in the brothels and low life taverns of Edinburgh, "in the companion of seamen, chimney sweeps and thieves", as he put it, which must have furnished abundant inspiration for the gallery of roguish characters he was to later create.

Whilst still in Edinburgh Stevenson got to know a one-legged Gloucestershire poet called William Henley, who had come to the city to seek medical advice from the famed Dr Lister and to try and save his leg from the ravages of TB. They became good friends with Stevenson saying, "there is something boisterious and piractical in his manner of talk... he will roar you down.. he will undergo passions of revolt and agony". In short, he was to become the template for the fictitious Long John Silver.

Needless to say his law studies did not survive long, although, in 1875, he did actually get called to the Bar. Three years later, to his father's great disapproval, he sailed to America to marry the love of his life, a divorced mother of two, Fanny Osborne.

His shocked parents, eventually reconciled to the match - and to the fact that their son was now devoted to the writing of horror and adventure tales rather than practising at the Bar - promised him an annual income of £250. Stevenson and his family (which now included a twelve year old stepson, Lloyd) returned to Scotland, where, encouraged by his magnanimous father, he began to write **Treasure Island** in 1881.

The frontispiece of the *Silverado Squatters* written in California before *Treasure Island*. The hero, Juan Silverado, was the inspiration for the name John Silver.

Stevenson, meanwhile, had been diagnosed with TB and it was recommended that he go to a Swiss clinic. Here he met John Addington Symonds, the gifted son of Dr Symonds, the Bristol writer and historian, who was to have a great influence upon him and whose character he was to celebrate in print. Could it be that whilst conversing with Symonds he began to toy with the idea of setting his yarn in Bristol - as well as using the names Trelawny and Smollett, both associated with the city.

At first the adventure story was serialized in a boy's magazine, *Young Folks* - under the pseudonym Captain George North - between October 1881 and January 1882. It only earned it's author, as he was to put it, "one hundred jingly jangly pounds" and initially attracted little attention.

However, when Stevenson revised it and published it in book form a year later, it captured the public's imagination. Since then it has never since been out of print and has been translated into many languages. There have been plays, films, television and radio adaptations, sequels, and even musicals, as well as notable illustrated editions.

Stevenson, who went on to write many more tales, travelled widely. He and Fanny eventually ended up on the island of Samoa on a plantation 600 feet above sea level, where he lived like a chieftain surrounded by his family and servants in a magnificent house designed by himself.

The author was known for his great hospitality and his visitors included missionaries, officials, officers from British warships and traders, plus Samoan chiefs and their retainers. These last gave him the name *Tusitala*, meaning Writer of Tales. When he died on December 3rd, 1884, forty Samoans cut a steep path up the mountainside and buried him, as he had wished, on the summit of Mount Vaea, where a memorial stands over his grave to this day.

The map that started it all. After two weeks of torrential rain in Braemar, Scotland, Stevenson and his father drew this treasure map to amuse themselves. From this Robert Louis Stevenson created *Treasure Island* itself. In "fifteen glorious days" half of the book had been written.

John Addington Symonds of Clifton Hill House, a famous Bristol historian and classicist, friend of Robert Louis Stevenson. On long cold winter nights he spoke of his home town to Stevenson, which possibly inspired him to make Bristol part of the setting of *Treasure Island*.

Bust of William Ernest Henley by Auguste Rodin. Stevenson based the character of Long John Silver on Henley.

Treasure Island Trail

..... Bristol .....

A. Blind Pew
B. The Captains Papers
C. Long John Silver
D. Jim Hawkins

Bristol Bridge

Harbour

Welsh Back

Baldwin Street

King Street

Island Trail

Blind Pew and Jim **Mervyn Peake, 1949**

The Bristol Treasure Island Trail

Ⓐ Blind Pew

The opening chapters of **Treasure Island** are set on the Devon coast at an inn called *The Admiral Benbow,* where young Jim Hawkins lives with his parents. The remoteness of the place attracts an old sea dog by the name of Billy Bones who, as it turns out, possesses a map showing the whereabouts of Cap'n Flint's treasure. Pirates up and down the coast are searching for him and one such fellow, Black Dog, eventually finds him.

After this rum-sodden Billy begins to confide in Jim. Then another pirate, Blind Pew, arrives on the scene, and when he hands Billy the infamous Black Spot, a sign that his days are numbered, the shock is enough to kill him. Before he dies however, and just before Blind Pew returns with his pirate band, he thrusts the treasure map into Jim's hands.

By now the lad had fortunately summoned help. Two mainstays of the community, Dr Livesey and Squire Trelawney with his men, turn up in the nick of time and set to with the pirates. Then, in the confusion that follows, Blind Pew is trampled to death.

The Trust has chosen **King St.** *for the start of the Treasure Island Trail because it's considered to be Bristol's most historic and atmospheric street. Not only does it contain Britain's oldest continuously working theatre, but it is also blessed with two ancient hostelries, both renowned for their sea-going associations - The Naval Volunteer and the Llandoger Trow.*

The Captain's Papers **Mervyn Peake, 1949**

Ⓑ *The Captain's Papers*

After the pirates have been scattered Jim admits to his rescuers what they have been searching for. Using the pirate map Squire Trelawney immediately starts to make plans to set sail and retrieve the treasure. Dr Livesey is concerned because the Squire is not known as a man who can keep a secret. The three then set off for Bristol Docks to find a ship.

Here, Dr Livesey's fears are confirmed. Despite securing a worthy ship - *The Hispaniola* - and engaging a good captain called Smollett, the Squire starts blabbing their plans around town. He then employs, as crew, a sea cook and - although he is unaware of it at the time - a pirate, by the name of Long John Silver. Much against Captain Smollett's wishes, Silver gets more and more of his old desperados on board as crew.

Half way along Harbourside's **Welsh Back***, between* **King Street** *and* ***The Hole in the Wall*** *pub, there is an opening amongst the dockside buildings where the officers of the Hispaniola would possibly have planned their voyage. This would have been done by many seafarers in this locality. This is also where merchant and seaman Woodes Rogers who lived in Queen Square, along with Bristol physician and second captain, Dr. Thomas Dover and West Country pilot William Dampier, would have fitted out their vessels, the* **Duke** *and* **Duchess,** *for their successful privateering trip to the Pacific in 1708.*

Long John Silver **Mervyn Peake, 1949**

ⓒ *Long John Silver*

Silver's Bristol dockside pub was the ***Spy-Glass Inn*** - and Jim was to meet him there. He recoils with horror when he discovers that the landlord has only one leg. Could this be the man, he thinks, that he was warned about?

The jovial Silver gets on well with just about everybody and before long not only has he befriended Jim but Trelawney has confided in him as well. The lad is fascinated by Silver's parrot, Cap'n Flint, who cries out "Pieces of Eight, Pieces of Eight".

Despite Jim spotting Black Dog in the Spy-Glass, he remains unaware of Silver 's dark side. The cook's choice of crew leads to a row between Cap'n Smollett and Squire Trelawney. The Captain says that he doesn't like the sound of the voyage OR the crew and that everyone in the port, except him, seems to know their destination. Cautious Smollett eventually puts to sea with firearms locked in the aft cabin.

*Many a Bristol inn has laid claims to be the Spy-Glass, but the only surviving pub that really fits the description is **Queen Square's The Hole in the Wall**. Situated on the quayside, with an entrance from different streets and even possessing its very own spy-hole feature, originally used as a look-out for the hated press gang, the pub offers everything, even a view across the river to Redcliffe.*

Jim in the apple barrel **Mervyn Peake, 1949**

⒟ *Jim Hawkins*

The ship sets sail with Mr Arrow, the first mate, suspicious of Silver and his cronies. He gives them a hard time and Long John has a job keeping the crew's tempers at bay, telling them that he is going to "take care" of Arrow.

He tempts the first mate with Plum Duff, complete with a double dose of rum. He then plies him with extra tots and during a storm he is washed overboard. The piratical crew are still not happy and plan to mutiny - but their plans are overheard by Jim while he is hiding in an apple barrel.

After land is sighted, Jim informs the squire, the doctor and the captain about the planned mutiny. The Squire realises just what a bad judge of character he's been.

Silver is in a long boat towing the Hispaniola to a safe anchorage when the pirates attack the officers. Silver calls one of the pirates, George Merry, "a blundering squid" for disobeying his orders.

*Alongside **Redcliffe Wharf,** by the bridge, and set amongst the dockside cobbles and hoists, the Trust would like to see a statue of Jim resting against some apple barrels and keeping a weather eye out for rascally Long John Silver. Using barrels would echo the days of Bristol as a working port.*

Ben Gunn meets Jim **Mervyn Peake, 1949**

ⓔ *Ben Gunn*

Just as the pirates gain the shore Jim runs away and escapes. He then runs into the marooned Ben Gunn who is frightened of Flint's men - and Long John Silver in particular. He tells Jim that, although he has stayed alive on goats and berries, he longs for some cheese. When Gunn realises that the lad isn't one of Flint's men they became friends and Gunn shows him a coracle he had made.

Meanwhile the Squire and the others have left the ship for the shore, leaving two men on board to keep the pirates out. But they were soon overpowered and the mutineers start firing on the Squire's party. They make their way to an old stockade where Jim is reunited with them and prepare to repel the inevitable pirate attack. Silver - after unsuccessfully attempting a truce - calls out "them that die'll be the lucky ones!". Smollett and some others attempt to chase off the pirates but receive shots in exchange. Several men on both sides are killed.

The men in the stockade are concerned that the pirates may bring up the Hispaniola and flatten the stockade with cannon fire. Without telling anyone Jim goes back to the Hispaniola, using Gunn's coracle, to stop them.

Redcliffe caves - one of Bristol's hidden treasures - have had many uses over the centuries and would be the natural haunt of someone like Gunn, emulating his cave-like home on Treasure Island. The caverns, which have spawned many legends - ranging from King Alfred's 9th century hideout to associations with smugglers and slaves, were mostly formed by the excavation of sand for the making of bottle glass during the 17th and 18th centuries. The sand was also used as ship's ballast and the caves as general storage by African traders.

Israel Hands plummets to his death **Mervyn Peake, 1949**

Ⓕ *Israel Hands*

Once back on board, Jim finds the ship guarded by just two pirates, both of whom are drunk and brawling. Jim's old enemy, Israel Hands, is the victor. He spots the lad and immediately sets out to kill him.

Jim escapes up the main mast, with Israel in pursuit. At the crow's nest, Jim can go no further and turns to face his foe. Israel throws his knife at him and, hitting him in the arm, pins him to the mast. Then the pistol Silver had given Jim goes off. It shoots Hands between the eyes and he crashes to his death. Jim then cuts the anchor line and, letting the Hispaniola drift across the bay, takes down the Jolly Roger and replaces it with the Union Jack. With the ship safe, he goes back to the stockade to meet up with his companions. Instead he ends up with Silver and his cutthroats.

Silver rescues Jim by pretending to take him hostage and then, under a flag of truce, gets Dr Livesey to tend his wound. The pirates disapprove and try to depose him as their leader. Silver outwits them, even after they have given him the Black Spot. Long John cunningly keeps a foot in both camps by pretending to keep Jim hostage, whilst siding with the doctor.

*At the entrance to the **Bathurst Basin**, and alongside one of Bristol's last remaining ancient slipways, the Trust would like to erect a ship's mast showing Israel Hands either chasing Jim up the mast with a knife in his mouth, or plummeting to his death. The Basin, before the construction of the Floating Harbour two hundred years ago, was known as Trin Mills pond and was where the Malago stream, coming from the Dundry slopes via Novers Hill, entered a still tidal river Avon. It was used by the Corporation for duck shoots and other entertainments.*

Treasure Island **Mervyn Peake, 1949**

Ⓖ *A Survivor*

Silver is still arguing with the crew about Jim. He accuses Merry, who wants to kill the lad, of being "brisk for business". Silver then takes Jim to one side and tells him that he's "as smart as paint". He produces the treasure map and then stands down as their leader. The pirates rush off to find the treasure.

Pointing the way on the macabre treasure trail are Flint's dead crew's corpses. The pirates are further "spooked" when they hear a ghostly voice (actually Ben Gunn) crying out the name of a former shipmate - "Darby McGraw".

They find an old sea chest but, after digging around, realise that the treasure is long gone. They then turn on their former leader and in the resulting fight Silver kills George Merry. He and Jim are then rescued by Livesey, Trelawney and their party - together with Ben Gunn. The castaway reveals that he has hidden the treasure in his cave and after rescuing the Squire's party takes them there as well.

You'll have to read Treasure Island for yourself if you want to know the ending...

*On **Merchants Landing**, perhaps guiding people from **Redcliffe Wharf** to the new **Museum of Bristol** on **Wapping Wharf**, the Trust would like to put a statue of an ordinary seaman carrying a load along the quayside - it could even be the treasure from Ben Gunn's cave. Even if you aren't on the trail it's a scene reminiscent of Bristol's maritime past.*

Bibliography

Albury, Paul. '*The Story of The Bahamas*' Macmillan Education Ltd 1975

Betty, J.H.'*Bristol Observed*' Redcliffe Press 1986

Brown, Harold G.'*Bristol, England*' Rankin Bros. Ltd. 1946

Cairney, John.'*The Quest for Robert Louis Stevenson*' Luath Press 2004

Craton, Michael.'*A History of the Bahamas*'(3rd Edition) San Salvador Press 1986

Dampier, William. '*A New Voyage Round the World*' London 1697

Defoe, Daniel. '*Robinson Crusoe*' London 1719

Earle, Peter '*The Pirate Wars*' Methuen 2003

Greenacre, Francis '*Maritime Artists of Bristol*' Redcliffe Press 1982

Hutton, Stanley '*Bristol and its Famous Associations*' J.W. Arrowsmith 1907

Johnson, Captain. '*General History of Ye Pyrates*' London 1724

Jones, Donald. '*Captain Woodes Rogers' Voyage Round the World*' Bristol Branch of the Historic Association 1992

Manwaring, G.E '*Woodes Rogers - Privateer and Governor*' Cassell and Co. Ltd 1928

Marley, David F. '*Pirates: Adventurers of the High Seas*' Arms and Armour Press 1995

McLynn, Frank '*Robert Louis Stevenson*' Hutchinson 1993

Nicholls, J.F. and Taylor, John. '*Bristol Past and Present Vols II and III*' J.W.Arrowsmith 1882

Norris, Gerald '*West Country Pirates and Buccaneers*' Dovecote Press 1990

Novak, Maximillian E '*Daniel Defoe - Master of Fictions*' Oxford University Press 2001

Preston, Diana and Michael. '*A Pirate of Exquisite Mind*' Doubleday 2004

Rogers, Woodes.'*A Cruising Voyage Round the World*' London 1712

Souhami, Diana.'*Selkirk's Island*' Weidenfeld & Nicholson 2001

Stevenson, Robert Louis.'*Treasure Island*' Cassell & Co. Ltd. 1883

Stevenson, Robert Louis.'*Treasure Island*' **Illustrated by Lyle Justis** Arden Book Co. 1930

Stevenson, Robert Louis. '*Treasure Island*' **Illustrated by Mervyn Peake** Eyre & Spotiswoode 1949

Swift, Jonathon '*Gullivers Travels*' London 1726

Pieces of Eight

The late Frank Shipsides, first patron of The Long John Silver Trust, handing over his painting of the famous *Hole In The Wall* (print 1 of 70), on Bristol's harbourside.